One
Is Enough

Written by Julie Kidd Cook
Illustrated by Melissa Iwai

Children's Press®
A Division of Scholastic Inc.
New York • Toronto • London • Auckland • Sydney
Mexico City • New Delhi • Hong Kong
Danbury, Connecticut

To Ellen, Lindsay, Martha, and Mary, who keep me writing
—J.K.C.

For Emily and her lovely fashion sense
—M.I.

Reading Consultant

Eileen Robinson
Reading Specialist

Library of Congress Cataloging-in-Publication Data

Cook, Julie Kidd, 1959-
   One is enough / written by Julie Kidd Cook ; illustrated by Melissa Iwai.
      p. cm. — (A Rookie reader)
   Summary: A girl is happy with one of everything, from a dog and a stick
to a shovel and a seed.
   ISBN 0-516-25152-X (lib. bdg.)   0-516-25283-6 (pbk.)
   [1. One (The number)—Fiction. 2. Stories in rhyme.] I. Iwai, Melissa, ill.
II. Title. III. Series.
   PZ8.3.C768On 2004
   [E]—dc22

                                                2004009329

CHILDREN'S PRESS, and A ROOKIE READER®, and associated logos are trademarks and or regi
tered trademarks of Scholastic Library Publishing. SCHOLASTIC and associated logos are trademarks and or registered trademarks of Scholastic Inc.
1 2 3 4 5 6 7 8 9 10 R 14 13 12 11 10 09 08 07 06 05

One is enough.

4

One dog. One stick.

6

One throw. One lick.
One is enough for me.

8

One branch. One tree.

One push. One whee!
One is enough for me.

One shovel.

One seed.

One book I read.
One is enough for me.

16

One dip. One drop.

18

One blow. One pop.
One is enough for me.

One chair. One cook.

One page. One book.

24

One is enough for me.

25

One kiss.

26

One light.

One hug good night.

One is enough for me.

Word List (30 words)

blow	enough	light	seed
book	for	me	shovel
branch	good	night	stick
chair	hug	one	throw
cook	I	page	tree
dip	is	pop	whee
dog	kiss	push	
drop	lick	read	

About the Author

Julie Kidd Cook lives in Prairie Village, Kansas, with her husband, Mark, and three children, Ian, Johanna, and Sarah. Julie has always loved the sound of words, their rhymes, and rhythms in stories and poems. She likes to play with words in her writer's notebook to see what happens. This story grew out of playing with the word one.

About the Illustrator

Melissa Iwai has illustrated nine books, including *Big Bad Wolf* and *The Great Stroller Adventure*, also published by Scholastic. She lives in Brooklyn, New York, with her husband Denis.